THE BURROWING OWL

The True Adventures of How a Family Found and Raised a Burrowing Owl

By Thomas J. Wood / Derrick J. Wood

This book is about a baby burrowing owl a family raised. The events and the story were taken from the journal the author and his family kept while they had the owl. We have used pages from the original journal with permission from the author and his family.

© Copyright 2018, 2019 Thomas Wood / Derrick Wood

Visit the Reggie website at **ReggieTheOwl.com**

Contact us at **info@reggietheowl.com**

Farabee Publishing, Chandler, AZ 85244
www.Farabeepublishing.com

Special thanks to Gerry Williams Jr for his editing the book from a 10-year-olds perspective.

All rights reserved. This book, or parts thereof, may not be reproduced in any form without permission.

ISBN: 978-1-64255-693-3
Library of Congress Control Number: 2018933431

Printed in the United States of America

*Book Cover designed by: Derrick J. Wood and Akivda M
Illustrations by Thomas J. Wood*

In Loving Memory of

Lexie Wood
and
Thomas Wood Jr.

CONTENTS

Preface

The story you are about to read is based on true events that happened some time ago—the late 1960s, to be exact.
I began writing these events down the day my son brought a baby burrowing owl home. Reggie, as we called him, lived with us for about a year and a half and never ceased to amaze us.

The burrowing owl is just one of nature's many extraordinary and beautiful creatures.

When fully grown, the burrowing owl stands at a charming height of 10 inches. That's about the span of a man's hand from the tip of the pinky, to the tip of the thumb.

The wing span is about 23 inches, which is about the length of a skateboard. Their average lifespan is seven years.

Most burrowing owls have creamy white chests, sandy brown heads and wings, and hundreds of black and white spots that freckle their backs and tails.

Preface

You can't miss their bright yellow eyes or their deep black pupils that grow large for hunting in the dark. Their legs are long and light brown and they sport four, dark chocolate brown toe nails on each of their mighty claws.

Instead of nesting in trees, they nest in burrows underground; hence, their name. Burrowing owls are the only bird of prey in North America to nest underground. Amazing, yes?

I had seen burrowing owls before at the San Diego Zoo, which was close to where we lived in Chula Vista, California.

I know it will be hard to imagine, but we didn't have the Internet in those days. You see, we weren't one hundred percent positive that what we had before us was an actual burrowing owl, and we couldn't go Online to do a quick search to confirm it.

We had what all families used back then— Encyclopedias. These books were full of knowledge and fascinating illustrations.

You had to flip through hundreds of pages to find the information you desired. And that is exactly what we did.

Every creature is distinguished by features unique to their own kind, and baby owls, or owlets, don't look anything like baby ducks or baby chickens.

We found our match and a burrowing owl he was. But really, it didn't matter—we were already in love.

Preface

Obviously, a burrowing owl ought to live in the wild and not in captivity. But what else can you do when a lost and helpless baby owlet arrives at your doorstep?

Well, I'll tell you that and more. This is the story about how one, little orphaned burrowing owl, brought five children and their parents together on a mission to care for him as best they could. And in doing so learned that—there's no such thing as an ordinary day with a burrowing owl around.

Though our days revolved around Reggie, it is the unique way Reggie impacted our once ordinary lives and those around us which makes this story such a special adventure.

I hope you will find it so as well.

T.J. Wood
Chula Vista
April, 2018

Chapter 1

A Ball of Fuzz

It was an autumn day in southern California, and the sun had just begun to set beyond the Pacific Ocean.

A cold wind blew, pushing the leaves across the school playground where Steve, our eldest son, walked along. He spotted a tiny ball of fuzz on the ground and stopped his foot, just in time, to avoid stepping on it.

Thank goodness, he did—that ball of fuzz turned out to be baby owl! Steve marveled at the tiny creature and wondered where it came from? He looked around for its family or maybe some kind of nest but didn't see anything.

Knowing the little owl didn't have much of a chance if left alone, he decided to pick it up and bring it home.

1

Reggie, the Burrowing Owl

(Isn't that what all little boys and girls do when they find a cute and helpless new pet— bring it home to mom and dad to help them save it?)

The baby owl fit snugly in the palm of Steve's hand. Its tiny body shivered with cold, so Steve unbuttoned his coat and tucked the owl, still in hand, close to his warm body to protect it from the cold wind.

And this is when our worlds collided. Three blocks of sprinting brought Steve busting through the front door exhausted and excited. Not stopping to catch his breath, he yelled, "Mom! Dad! Look what I found! It's a tiny baby owl. I almost stepped on it. Can we keep it?"

Not waiting for an answer, Steve marched into the living room, knelt on the carpet, and removed the owl from his coat. In a moment, the rest of the family came rushing in around Steve to see what he had. It was something with a big head and big eyes!

It looked surprisingly like a ball of soft peach fuzz. "What? An owl? No way! So cute!" We were instantly enamored.

A Ball of Fuzz

The kids—Debbie, Bill, Linda, and Tom Jr, my wife, Lexie, and I were just as excited as Steve.

We were all kneeling on the floor petting the baby owl, when Debbie yelled, "We have to give it a name!" Everyone threw out ideas, and in the end, we agreed on the one Lexie liked best—Reggie.

We didn't know if it was a boy, or girl, but by golly—we were now the family of a burrowing owl named, Reggie!

Then reality set in. How do we take care of a burrowing owl, or any wild creature for that matter? Encyclopedia to the rescue!

The kids looked up owls and found the one that matched Reggie's markings.

We were thrilled to learn we were the proud new parents of a beautiful, bouncing, baby burrowing owl or as baby owls are known as an owlet.

Lexie and I made a promise to the children to do our best to keep Reggie alive, but we also let them know our concerns. This was not a domesticated animal like a dog or cat, and anything we did, would be a gamble. The children seemed to understand what we were trying to say.

Reggie, the Burrowing Owl

Not knowing what a burrowing owlet liked to eat, we decided to start with broken pieces of white bread, soaked in warm milk.

But Reggie would have nothing to do with that! All he did was squawk and give us a dirty look.

Next, Lexie tried chewing some of the bread. She placed it in a spoon, then gently opened Reggie's beak and slid it inside.

To our surprise, he ate it! But he sure made a mess in the process. Reggie closed his eyes and shook his head tossing milk and mushy bread all over himself, even getting it in his eyelashes.

We kept working the chewed milk-soaked bread, into his tiny beak, stifling our laughter at the ridiculous sight of him.

Reggie soon tired of milk and bread. "Okay, what next?" we asked each other. Reggie was walking out of the towel we had him in and giving us the stink eye.

Later, I learned owls sometimes look mean but do not act mean. In other words, owls might look angry, but they aren't.

A Ball of Fuzz

We figured Reggie was still hungry, so I went to the refrigerator and took out some baloney. I tore off a small piece, held it to Reggie's beak, and before you could say, "Boo!" Reggie grabbed it from my fingers and gulped it down. Almost as soon as Reggie ate the piece of baloney, he started acting strangely, which really scared us.

Reggie looked right at me. His pupils were grew bigger, then smaller, then big again, and small again. He began to lose his balance, wobbling back and forth. He looked about to fall over.

I quickly placed my hand next to Reggie to steady him, but whatever was happening stopped. Thankfully, Reggie was normal again.

I said, "Maybe Reggie isn't going to make it. He's too weak, or maybe being around humans like this is a shock to such a little creature," all the while hoping I was wrong.

I decided to give Reggie another piece of baloney, he ate it and again the same thing happened. Sadly, everyone thought the same thing at that point— something was indeed wrong, and our little Reggie was not going to live long.

Reggie, the Burrowing Owl

"Wait a minute!" I said. "Maybe this baloney is too cold for little Reggie to swallow!" I warmed up the baloney and gave him another piece.

Reggie gulped it down without any problems. "Hurray!" we shouted. He ate several more pieces of baloney and drank some warm water.

Once he appeared satisfied with his meal, we placed Reggie in a shoebox on a soft towel. Without making a sound, Reggie went fast to sleep.

I could only guess that in a way, perhaps, Reggie knew in our home, he would be loved and well cared for. We all sighed in relief knowing he had a full belly and a cozy bed, and maybe—just maybe—Reggie would be okay after all. But we still nervously wondered, would he make it through the first night?

Chapter 2

Things That Go Screech in the Night

Do you remember bringing home your first kitten or puppy and waking up in the wee hours of the morning to strange sounds in an otherwise quiet house?

The noises were, of course, the whimpers of your new pet. Well, it was between 2:00 and 3:00 a.m. when a real high pitch screech penetrated the silence of our house.

I bolted awake, sitting straight up in bed. I moved so fast I woke Lexie, my wife.

"What's wrong?" she asked, still half asleep.

"Did you hear that?" I asked.

"Hear what?" she said.

Reggie, the Burrowing Owl

I listened for a moment but only heard the wind blowing through the trees. Then, there it was again! The strange noise that woke me up.

"That! Did you hear that?" I said.

In my drowsiness, I forgot there was a new baby animal in the house.

Then I realized, "Hey, that's Reggie crying!" We rushed down the stairs flipping on lights as we went. We headed for the living room, where we'd left Reggie snoozing, in a shoebox near the fireplace.

What a sight to see, there was the shoebox alright, and all we saw was this tiny head of fuzz popping out, with big eyes and a wide-open beak.

Things That Go Screech in the Night

If I hadn't heard it for myself, I wouldn't have believed that such a loud screech could come from such a tiny creature—but boy did it!

By now the whole family, except for the baby, Tom Jr., were once again huddled around Reggie. I picked Reggie up, while still in the towel and gently stroked his head.

Instead of a wagging tail or a soft purr, Reggie closed his eyes in contentment, showing off his long lashes.

His beak was still wide open, but his screech was less piercing than before. We thought little Reggie was hungry again.

We warmed more milk and soaked pre-chewed bread bits in it to feed him. After eating, we cleaned Reggie off because—remember—he shook and flung the milk-soaked food all over himself when he ate.

(It turned out Reggie's messy eating behavior was to be the norm. He did not outgrow it until he was older.)

Next, we gave Reggie some warm water to drink, and he seemed content.

Content meaning—he wasn't screeching anymore! Reggie closed his eyes and was soon sound asleep.

"Alright," I said, "let's all get back to bed and join Reggie in sleeping, while we can!" At least until 7:00 a.m. that is!

Chapter 3

The Breakfast Club

The whole family was up, and ready for breakfast. "Good morning," I said, to my five, now six children. Reggie was awake, and we let him out of the shoebox, onto the living room carpet.

Reggie, the Burrowing Owl

We felt good seeing him scamper around the floor. He looked healthy and lively like a burrowing owl in the wild; except, this was in our home, on the living room floor!

It was feeding time again and oh yes there was the same cleanup. If ever there was a messy eater, it was our Reggie!

He was as curious about life as our son Tom Jr.

The Breakfast Club

Everything was new to him, and Reggie had to check everything out—I mean everything! We watched him scamper about and explore eventually finding his way over to where Tom Jr., our ten-month-old, was lying on the living room floor.

They both just stared and studied each other for a long time. A baby of the wild and a human baby, looking at each other—that was a sight to see!

Next, Reggie did his march through the living room, again. We watched this fuzzy ball of an owl, boldly approach the sliding glass door, but to his surprise (and ours), he jumped back in alarm, and let out a squawk.

We all laughed as we realized Reggie was surprised by his reflection! Reggie continued his investigation, under the coffee table, over to the sofa, under the chairs, and back again.

At first, we thought he was trying to find a way out, but he ended the exploration by his little shoebox nest. Lexie picked him up and held him close.

Reggie stood in the palm of her hand and looked around. Lexie placed Reggie tenderly back in the shoebox on the soft towel. He ruffled around, until he found a comfortable spot, then snuggled down and fell fast asleep. Taking in a new environment is exhausting work!

Chapter 4

Kids Will Be Kids

Caring for, and raising, a baby owl along with five children, and one still in diapers, proved to be an adjustment and challenge—to say the least. Tom Jr. wanted to play with Reggie and would not stay away.

We worried about Reggie getting hurt, so to help teach Tom Jr. gentleness, we held Reggie and supervised while Tom Jr. pet him. Soon enough, Tom Jr. was just as calm and gentle as could be.

As for the other children, well they wanted to try and outdo each other in taking care of Reggie. I believe they were trying to see who could get Reggie to like them the best.

Reggie, the Burrowing Owl

Linda and Bill argued over who should be the one to feed Reggie. Steve felt Reggie belonged to him since he was the one who found him and used this to argue for his right to feed Reggie.

Ultimately though, it was Lexie, who while taking care of Tom Jr. at the same time, did most of the feeding in the beginning.

We let Reggie roam the living room during the day, and whenever he was tired, he'd waddle over to his shoebox. Whoever saw him, would scoop him up and put him to bed.

One of the funny habits Reggie acquired while in the living room, was to jump out from under the chair and grab at your leg.

The first time, it scared the peanuts out of us! But we soon learned to anticipate it, and make sure not to step on the little guy. He wasn't trying to hurt anyone. I guess it was like a game for him. And so, we nicknamed him, the "bird hound."

We did try to warn any visiting friends or family members, but even then, they'd have the surprise of their lives, and we witnessed some hilarious reactions.

As the end of our first week living with a baby burrowing owl came to a close, we realized how we had come together as a family to keep Reggie alive.

We'd been hoping against hope, he'd be okay, and to our happy surprise, he was both alive and thriving.

To help with the feedings, we bought an eye dropper and used it to give Reggie warm milk, pre-chewed bits of bread, warm baloney and water.

Reggie continued to eat, make a mess, and we would clean him up, then repeat the whole process.

Though Reggie couldn't fly yet, he stomped and waddled everywhere on the ground, like the marching fuzzball he was.

On our seventh night with Reggie, the family gathered together and laughed and talked about all the wonderful things that happened over the past week.

Reggie, the Burrowing Owl

Our eldest daughter Debbie asked, "Do you think Reggie is happy being with us?"

"Yes, Deb," I said, "I believe so. After all, Reggie's part of the family now and the rest of the family is happy!"

Lexie and I tucked the kids into bed and smiled to ourselves, thankful for such a rewarding week together.

We had welcomed a new family member into our hearts and home. We'd learned a lot already, but realized there was more to learn and much to enjoy.

Chapter 5

Growing Pains
Feathers and Refrigerators, Oh My!

Over the next several weeks the morning routine was the same, except on the weekends. Everyone would be up by 6:00 a.m., Lexie would feed Reggie, then I would talk and play with him before going to work, and the kids would do the same before leaving for school.

After everyone left for the day Lexie let Reggie run loose in the living room. This helped Reggie became comfortable in his surroundings.

Reggie, the Burrowing Owl

On the weekends, Reggie ruled the roost so to speak, meaning he had everyone's undivided attention. The children spoiled Reggie, and I believe he knew it!

The whole family loved the little owl, and we didn't mind he had us all wrapped around his little finger, er, talon.

Playtime with Reggie included either strolling by the chair he hid under and being attacked by the "ferocious" bird hound or tossing a light dish towel on top of him.

The towel made him screech and then slowly, very slowly, he'd stick his head out from under it, to see who did it and give them "the look" with those big eyes!

Both games left everyone in a fit of giggles. Living with a wild creature, especially a bird of prey, left us in constant awe and wonder.

It'd been about four weeks since Reggie came to our home, and to our knowledge, he'd never ventured anywhere outside of the living room—until this Saturday morning.

After the kids had their playtime with Reggie, he followed Lexie, without her knowing, into the kitchen.

She was startled by a loud screech and immediately turned to see the little guy standing right behind her.

Growing Pains
Feathers and Refrigerators, Oh My!

He looked up and let out another screech. What happened next, was one of many comical events we had the privilege of experiencing.

The refrigerator motor turned on behind Reggie, and he did an immediate about-face, staring down the enormous metal monster.

He flapped his little wings, let out one of his loudest screeches, then high-tailed it out of there! But our brave Reggie wasn't to be bested by any metal monster.

He crept back toward the kitchen, hiding behind the edge of a wall, and slowly peeked his little head around the corner. His eyes narrowed on the refrigerator. His pupils got real big.

Reggie bent over and looked about ready to charge, but instead, he crept stealthily over to the refrigerator. He stopped in front of it and let out another ear-piercing screech.

Apparently, his satisfaction was complete. He'd triumphed. He'd shown that monstrous metal creature he wasn't scared! Now that he had sufficiently frightened the beast, Reggie decided it was safe to check out the rest of this new location called, the kitchen.

Without paying any attention to Lexie, he did his exploring, seem to tire, and returned to his shoebox in the living room. I picked Reggie up and sat down in my TV lounge chair.

I placed Reggie on my lap and began stroking his little head, back, and chest with my index finger. When I put my finger next to his chest, he perched on it.

Growing Pains
Feathers and Refrigerators, Oh My!

He always did enjoy a good beak and between-the-eyes rub. Perhaps Reggie's idea of love was a good cuddle?

I'm just so amazed that humans and animals, even wild animals, can interact. Even so, we must not forget that some animals are wild, and will always retain certain instincts that they can and do revert to.

Over the next few days, we noticed Reggie beginning to change. His peach fuzz started to disappear, and actual feathers took their place. I must say, he looked a little mangy during this process. Plus, it made a mess.

"Get ready," I thought, "things are going to become even more interesting around here. And real soon!"

Chapter 6

Lost and Found

It'd been nearly two months of unforgettable moments with Reggie, but there was one day, that would always stand out in our minds.

It was a Sunday. I was sleeping in late exhausted from a busy week. I awoke to loud voices downstairs. It sounded like the kids were arguing amongst themselves.

I quickly splashed some water on my face then ran down the stairs. I found the kids and Lexie looking under the sofa, behind the TV, and around the refrigerator.

"What's going on guys?" I asked.

Reggie, the Burrowing Owl

Lexie turned to me with a worried look on her face. Linda was crying. Steve was down on all fours looking under things and mumbling to himself.

Debbie sat at the kitchen table yelling, "It's not my fault!"

"Little Reggie is gone, Tom!" Lexie said.

"What! What do you mean gone?" I said.

"Well, Debbie was up first, went out to the back yard, when she came inside the house, Steve was up. Steve had gone to see Reggie, but Reggie wasn't in his shoebox, so Steve blamed Debbie!"

Everyone was upset, including me. We took the search outside and looked under the cars and around trees and plants.

I feared a cat or dog might have snatched Reggie if he had indeed wandered outside and into a neighbor's yard. He was still so small and looking for him was like looking for a needle in a haystack.

After several hours of searching, we had to accept that little Reggie was really, truly gone. Well, you can imagine our sadness and disappointment.

There was nothing but long faces all around. We gathered in the living room, and each person plopped down in silence filled with sadness.

Lost and Found

I let out a big sigh and was about to say something when an all too familiar loud screech broke the silence! It was a "Reggie screech" for sure.

You guessed right, if you imagined we all jumped up in the excitement and raced toward the sound of that lovable screech. We discovered Reggie standing by the stairs. Relief flooded our hearts.

"Oh, there's our baby!" Lexie said picking him up and kissing his head.

Reggie, the Burrowing Owl

The only places Reggie was familiar with were the living room and the land of the kitchen. Clearly, he was taking more of an interest in exploring this human habitat, or I suppose one could say, this human-sized burrow.

We'd changed Reggie's diet to lunch meat and hamburger as he grew, but we hadn't thought to change his bed.

This little scare confirmed we needed to provide something else, so Reggie couldn't just wander about getting lost or stepped on.

We went out that day and bought a standard, pink bird cage for Reggie to sleep in at night.

With a dish towel covering the top, this was just the perfect place for him to fall asleep in peace, and the best way for us to know the little guy wouldn't turn up lost again.

Wow, what a day! It's a great example of how families work together when one member is in trouble.

Steve, even apologized to Debbie, for making her feel bad when we couldn't find him.

Thank goodness, Reggie was safe once more.

Chapter 7

Reggie and the Baby

What a beautiful day it was, not a cloud in the sky. The sun was up, and I could hear birds singing outside. Even though it was still early morning, I knew it would be a warm day. What I didn't know was how exciting things were about to become. Changes were ahead for Reggie and the family.

All the big kids were gone, and it was just Lexie, Tom Jr. and me at the house. Oh, and of course Reggie.

Reggie, the Burrowing Owl

Reggie lost all his adorable peach fuzz and was complete with full-grown feathers now. He was a bit taller too. His most common facial expression, I later learned was a mean look.

I wondered if Reggie had the ability to look mean whenever he wanted? It was like he wanted to intimidate you before taking action.

Other times, he'd show affection by closing his eyes and kissing you on your cheek or nibbling on your finger.

When he'd get that "mean" look though I'd think, "Can I trust him?" I thought mostly about this at bedtime when I needed to put Reggie in the pink cage. What bird likes to be caged?

When I finally caught him, he'd put up some resistance, climbing the cage interior and screeching.

Once I placed the towel over the cage, he'd quiet down—sometimes! Despite all the commotion, he hadn't hurt any of us yet— thank goodness!

One morning, Lexie and I were listening to music while we watched Tom Jr. and Reggie play together. How exactly does a ten-month-old play with a bird of prey you ask?

Reggie and the Baby

Well, Reggie would stand still on the floor and Tom would crawl to him. Right before Tom could reach out to grab him, Reggie would suddenly hop out of Tom's reach!

Then, Tom would crawl to him again, and Reggie would hop away at the last second!

They repeated this little routine several times until Reggie had led Tom all over the living room. Tom Jr. would become frustrated when he couldn't get to Reggie.

Instead of getting angry or crying, he'd decide, "Okay, fine! I'll go back to playing with my toys."

So, he'd turn his back on Reggie and ignore him. I don't think Reggie liked that one bit.

He'd stare at Tom Jr. and then turn his head very quickly, left to right, like he was saying, "No, no!".

Then the best part. Reggie would get into his prowler pose. He'd bend his body just slightly and slowly sneak up on Tom Jr. When Reggie was right behind him, he'd grab ahold of Tom's diaper and pull while letting out a squawk.

Tom Jr. would laugh and laugh. When he turned around Reggie would jump back two or three feet, and the game would start all over again. We had fun just watching it all.

Later we would recall these events as they lead to what happened next.

The game didn't last long as Tom Jr. was getting sleepy. Lexie put him down for a nap and then returned to the living room. Reggie was still running around.

He'd go squawk at his reflection in the sliding glass door, and then run over to Lexie and squawk at her as if to scold her.

Chapter 8

Look, It's a Bird! It's a Plane! It's Reggie!

Well, right after one of these silly squawks, the front door burst open with a bang and Bill ran in yelling, "Can I have something to eat?"

His entrance made Lexie and me jump. But it made Reggie do a little more. In his surprise, Reggie let out a loud screech and jumped into the air with wings flapping.

Reggie, the Burrowing Owl

To his and our surprise, he just kept going up and up. Reggie was flying, flying in our living room! He went up and over to the couch next to Lexie and landed.

Reggie did a little dance-march-combo on the couch, flapped his wings, screeched, and flew up to the curtain rod. He perched on the curtain rod above the sliding door and looked down at us.

He let out another squawk and flew to the lampshade. Then, back to the curtain rod.

We were amazed. Sure, it's only natural a bird should fly, but we were so used to Reggie, well, just walking around everywhere. It was a strange turn of events.

If it hadn't been for Bill's loud entrance, would Reggie have tried to fly on his own? How do owls learn in the wild? We sure didn't know!

As I watched him fly excitedly from perch to perch, I couldn't help but think about how once baby humans learn to walk—they want to run!

When Bill slowed down long enough to realize we weren't rushing to make him any lunch, he ran into the living room only to see Reggie perched on the curtain rod!

"How long has Reggie been able to fly?" he asked, his jaw halfway to the ground.

Look, It's a Bird! It's a Plane! It's Reggie!

"Well Bill," Lexie answered, "he started to fly the moment you burst into the house. You scared the pants off us! And Reggie too—if he had pants."

"Wow, I made Reggie fly! Cool! Can I go and tell the others?"

"Sure," I said, "but go out slowly and quietly and please close the screen door."

Always the jokester, Bill stood up as slowly as humanly possible and acted the goof while tippy-toeing through the living room and out the front door.

After making sure the front screen was oh-so-gently closed, we heard him tear down the driveway yelling, "Debbie! Steve! Linda! Reggie can fly!"

In just minutes, it sounded like we had a stampede of elephants rushing toward our door. But these elephants could shout!

"You're making this up!"

"No, I'm not!"

"If you're lying, I'm gonna punch you in the nose!"

Then we heard Bill yell, "Wait! Mom and Dad said to come in slowly or we'll scare Reggie. And make sure to close the screen."

Reggie, the Burrowing Owl

Reggie can fly!

Look, It's a Bird! It's a Plane! It's Reggie!

So, they came in marching quietly and slowly. The room filled with the same excitement that was there the very the first day Reggie arrived at our home.

Now that Reggie had found his wings, we couldn't stop him. He was going from the living room to the kitchen, to the hall and back again and again.

Then, just like a helicopter, he hovered above my head and slowly descended. Yes, he landed on me!

"Okay," I said, as calmly as I could! I was startled by his talons digging into my scalp. I knew he didn't dig them in too deep because, thank goodness, I wasn't bleeding! It seemed, he just wanted to make sure not to slip.

Next, Reggie bent down, grabbed some of my hair with his beak, and started whittling away on the strands.

It tickled plenty, and I tried to compose myself, so I wouldn't laugh too hard and scare him. Since birds use their beaks to clean their feathers, I guessed Reggie thought my hair needed a good cleaning.

When he finished with me, he took turns and flew to another mop of hair, cleaned it, and then to another and another. Was he looking for our approval now that he could fly?

Reggie, the Burrowing Owl

Reggie flew around, off and on, for hours before he finally perched again on the curtain rod.

"Okay, new house owl rules," I said. "No running, make sure to close all doors, and for goodness sake, look when you sit because you never know where he'll be at any moment."

It was really "fun" to try and catch him at bedtime now! Before, I merely placed some hamburger in one hand and caught him with my free hand. No problem.

But he was too smart for that old gimmick now! And of course, he never did want to go to bed. He was an owl after all. Now that he could fly and liked to perch high on the curtain rod, all the rules were out the window.

I approached him with the hamburger, then I walked over to the sofa, and then to the lampshade, and back to the curtain rod.

Reggie had his fun by flying off screeching and not cooperating with me. In the end, it took both Lexie and me sitting in our chairs, holding a piece of hamburger, and pretending not to care what he did.

Then, just as pretty as you please, Reggie flew over to Lexie and landed in her lap for the piece of hamburger. I caught him quickly, but gently with one hand on his chest and the other on his back.

Look, It's a Bird! It's a Plane! It's Reggie!

He fussed, and screeched, and flapped as I placed him back into the pink cage. Not his favorite place to be. Nowhere near as grand as a curtain rod.

With Reggie finally in the cage, Lexie placed some fresh water and a nice big chunk of hamburger inside. Once she placed the towel over his cage, it only took a couple of minutes for all to be quiet again.

Wow, what a day. We went from Reggie on the floor pulling on Tom Jr's diaper to Reggie flying around the house and styling everyone's hair!

What more could one family ask for? We felt privileged to be around a wild creature living in "our" habitat, and happy he had adapted so well—so far!

He had not been aggressive up to that point, but now that he was flying, uh, well, we'd see! Reggie indeed found his wings that day.

But our family once again found something too—the excitement of being together, loving and feeling so close to one of God's marvelous creatures.

We continued to be amazed at how one little life can have so much impact. Who would have thought?

Chapter 9

Just the Two of Us

It was a quiet night. It was so quiet you could hear the house making creaking sounds. Everyone was in bed, including myself, but I couldn't sleep.

I just tossed and turned. Well, after one too many tosses and turns, I thought, "The heck with this," and quietly rolled out of bed.

I pulled on my robe and headed downstairs for a very early morning cup of coffee. I know, it doesn't seem like the best beverage to choose if you want to go back to sleep.

Reggie, the Burrowing Owl

With coffee in hand, I settled down in my TV chair and turned on the lamp next to me. As I quietly sat, I could hear the kids sleeping—okay, snoring!

I had nearly finished my drink, so I went back for a second cup, and I turned the radio on low for some music. I was about to sit in my chair when I heard a faint squawk, or was it a squeak? I guess I shouldn't have been surprised Reggie would wake up, with someone stirring about.

His little squawk was like someone whispering, "Psst! Hey buddy, look over here!" It was like he knew everyone else was asleep and he needed to "keep the noise down."

I thought, "Why not let Reggie out. Maybe he'd like a cup of coffee, too!" I removed the dish towel and opened the door.

At first, all he did was stare at me and quickly turn his head from one side to other, but the next moment, he flew out the door and onto the lamp shade.

I sat back down in my TV chair and continued listening to the soft music. To my surprise and delight, Reggie flew onto my left shoulder.

Just the Two of Us

He proceeded to whittle at my robe, moving up closer to my ear, until he was "nibbling" on my ear lobe.

While Reggie was going at it on my ear lobe, he made these soft, cute noises. If dogs wag their tails and cats purr, then owls quietly crackle and squeak when happy!

Perhaps this is true of all our fine-feathered friends. Either way, it remains one of the sweetest sounds I've ever heard.

Reggie nibbled on my ear lobe for a long time. Now and then he'd lean against my head and take a whittle at my sideburns, too.

In the wild, most owls sleep during the day and hunt at night. With Reggie living in our habitat, and adapting to our schedules, I realized it was possible for a wild creature to change their natural habits.

Reggie was a wild animal and needed to be respected. With Reggie perched on my shoulder, whittling and making soft noises, I questioned, "Is it wrong to keep him? Maybe we should let him go?"

I reasoned he had been with and handled by humans long enough now, that he might not last long in the wild on his own. He had developed a trust of humans, and that would not be to his advantage in the wild.

Reggie, the Burrowing Owl

Not all humans are kind to their fellow creatures; I didn't want anyone to harm Reggie.

Would he be able to hunt for food? He'd never had to! Yes, you are correct if you think I was making up all kinds of reasons to keep Reggie.

I didn't want to say goodbye to him, but I also wished we could let him return to the wild to live in freedom as God intended.

One might say, "Well, wild creatures become lost from the nest all the time around the world and do not survive. Don't worry about it!" and that would be correct to a point.

This baby owl (not such a baby anymore) was lost from his nest and then found in our world! We felt blessed to care for him and earn his love, but I often wished he could fly free in the big, blue sky from perch to perch.

Just then, Reggie dropped down onto my lap. He let out another tiny squawk while turning his head back and forth and looked at me as if to say, "So? Are you going to rub my head or not?"

I rubbed his head and he closed his eyes for a few seconds. Then I gently pinched his beak, between my thumb and index finger, and he lifted his left foot and grabbed my index finger. He could have pierced my finger easily with those claws, but he was amazingly gentle.

Just the Two of Us

He nibbled on my finger for a moment and then flew to his cage. Yes, you read that right, his cage!

He went inside, ate some raw hamburger, and drank some water, all while watching to see if I was coming over to close the door.

I stood still and watched him. Once he finished, he climbed out of the cage and flew into the dining room, perching somewhere dark. I couldn't see him.

I called to him, he flew into the living room and perched on the curtain rod.

"Come over here, Reggie," I said, but he just sat there staring.

"Reggie, come here," I said again, tapping on my left shoulder.

He stared a bit longer then flew to my shoulder, landed and walked down into my lap. So, there you go. Instead of a "lap dog," we had a "lap owl!"

When I sat in my chair, I liked to keep my ankles crossed and my feet resting on the footstool. Because I was still in my robe, the bottom section of my legs was exposed as they descended onto the footstool.

Reggie, the Burrowing Owl

After our "lap owl" snuggled for a bit, he took the path toward my feet.

Once he stepped off my robe and onto my bare skin, he wasn't as steady! He didn't grip my leg hard enough to hurt me, only tickle a lot!

Just the Two of Us

Reggie was trying to keep from slipping back and forth, as he balanced along my leg. I guess, my leg simulated a tree limb.

Well, he made it. Where? To my foot—my big toe to be exact! He did his best to not dig his talons deeply into my big toe, as he maintained his balance.

If he hadn't, the whole house would've known—if you catch my drift!

Here was a sight to behold, a burrowing owl perched on my big toe like the king of the hill.

He stayed there a moment looking at me, even letting out another little squawk. I called to him and tapped on my lap.

Reggie made the trek across my foot, walked upon my slippery leg, traversing the cushy robe, and returning to my lap.

I gently blew on his face and stroked his head and back. He settled down and closed his eyes, while I continued holding him.

There we were just the two of us, relaxed, comfortable and enjoying each other's company while listening to the radio playing low.

As I turned off the lamp, I saw there was a soft, early morning light peeking through the curtains. "Sunrise won't be long," I thought. We soon drifted off to sleep—even after two cups of coffee!

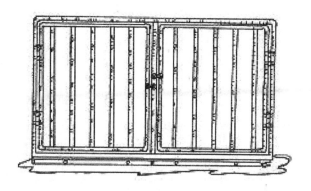

Chapter 10

The Rabbit Cage

Days turned into weeks, and weeks turned into months. Time was flying, just like Reggie flying past my head to the curtain rod each night.

The routine was the same. Lexie let Reggie out of his cage every morning, and I had the fun of putting him to bed. However, now that Reggie was an expert flier it was harder and harder to put him in his cage.

My old trick of ignoring him, to coax him to fly over to me, was no longer working.

Tempting him with a piece of hamburger meat wasn't working either. What was a parent to do?

Reggie, the Burrowing Owl

Here's an example of what I mean. In our kitchen, there was a wide-open space between the top of the cabinets and the ceiling.

Reggie loved to fly from one cabinet top to the next—way out of my reach. I'd stand on a chair tempting him with meat in one hand and trying to grasp him with the other. During the process, I was careful.

Once I finally had a hold of him, he would, naturally, squeak, squawk and screech while clawing the air and giving me that mean look. If I were in this situation, I'd probably do the same thing.

Reggie wanted to stay free, and since that is only natural, I couldn't blame him. As I brought him to his cage, I realized another issue. It was getting harder to fit both my hand and Reggie through the cage door. Either the cage was shrinking, or Reggie was growing.

My guess was the latter. Reggie had officially outgrown his cage. Time for a newer and bigger cage!

Our whole family went looking for the perfect cage. Perfect meant it was not only big enough for Reggie to stretch his wings inside but that it also looked nice while displayed in the living room. At first we had no luck.

The Rabbit Cage

But the next day, I told my fellow work buddies about my problem with Reggie's cage. They had known about Reggie from the start.

One of my good buddies, Harry, who was an ol' farm boy and horse trader said, "Tom, I have just the thing, that I think will work."

"Oh yeah?" I said. He told me he had a rabbit cage with a "double door" opening. After work, I went to Harry's house to see the cage. It was perfect. I paid Harry ten dollars and brought it home to show the family. They were very pleased.

Would Reggie feel the same?

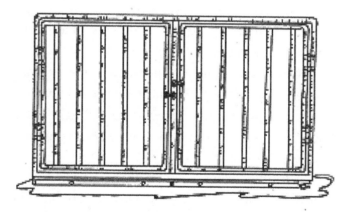

The cage was the length of a board, about three feet long. It was about two feet high and two feet wide. It had a double door that took up nearly the entire front of the cage and opened outward.

Reggie, the Burrowing Owl

We painted it a flat black, placed a dowel rod from one corner to the opposite corner, and set it on the floor, with paper beneath it. It was the same spot where the old pink cage and shoebox used to be. It was Reggie's spot.

It was time to look for Reggie and see how he liked his new digs. I went off to fetch him and when I found him, I placed him gently in his new cage.

He went from end to end checking everything out. Then, he sprang up onto the wooden dowel and flapped his wings like a proud eagle, or in this case an owl.

Oh, yeah. There was plenty of room! He wholeheartedly approved of the new cage—well, at least for its size.

Okay, now that we got Reggie's new digs ironed out the next big question was, "How can we train a wild bird of prey to go willingly to his cage each night without the hassle of chasing him all over the house?"

An idea came sooner than expected. A couple nights later Reggie was up to his old tricks, flying into the kitchen then into the living room, landing upon the curtain rod, and then over to the lampshade.

The Rabbit Cage

Back and forth, back and forth. While I watched TV, Reggie watched Lexie make dinner. He sat on top of the kitchen cabinet fixated on her every move.

Well, this made Lexie suspicious. Whenever she glanced up at him, he was staring down at her, with a mean look.

It must have been the smell of food because Reggie unexpectedly flew out of the kitchen, zooming past me, and landed on the floor.

He glanced at me for half a second, then walked right inside his new cage, through the open door. I repeat, Reggie willingly walked inside his cage.

Wow, I could not have planned it better. He snacked on leftovers he'd stashed inside the cage. I just couldn't believe it as I watched him.

After his snack, he walked over toward my chair, and flew up into my lap.

We just stared at each other. He had food all over his beak and eyelashes. I cleaned off his face like any good parent would, and then rubbed his chest. He gave a sweet little screech and whittled at his feathers.

Reggie, the Burrowing Owl

"Dinner time!" Lexie called. I set Reggie down on the floor, so I could go wash up and sit down at the table, for our meal with all the kids. Reggie flew into the kitchen and perched on a cabinet where he could watch us.

I tapped on the table and called to him. To my surprise, Reggie flew—not to the table—but to my shoulder.

Lexie held a piece of roast beef to his beak, and he nibbled it. He didn't gulp it down like usual, but we could tell he liked it.

He ate a few more pieces and then he flew over to his new cage, walked inside, and took a drink of water. Twice in the same night!

After dinner, Reggie joined us as we gathered in the living room to watch TV. He perched on the lamp shade.

Throughout the entire episode, Reggie kept flying down to the floor in front of the TV and walking back and forth squawking at it.

Then he'd fly back to the lampshade. Then down to the floor. He didn't stop until the show was over. Who knows, maybe he wasn't a fan of car chases?

The kids went to bed and Lexie was preparing Reggie's food for the night.

I said, "Hey Lexie, I want to try something. Please bring me Reggie's food on a saucer."

The Rabbit Cage

Lexie brought his food, and I placed the saucer on the floor of the cage.

I tapped on the bottom a couple of times and then walked away.

"I sure hope this works," I said, fingers crossed.

Reggie was on his curtain rod perch the whole time, watching and studying the situation.

Then whoosh! He flew to the floor in front of his cage, gave us a look and ran inside, pouncing on his food.

I rushed over to close the doors as he gave a squawk. We placed a big towel over the entire cage, so it was officially lights out!

"Wow!" we thought to ourselves. "We're becoming pretty good at training a wild animal." At least, that's what we thought. It didn't always work out like we hoped—believe me!

Chapter 11

Problems Will Arise—It's a Wild Animal!

Every living creature has habits and behaviors which affect others, either good or bad. Reggie was no different, especially since he was a wild bird of prey. From the time he began flying and moved into a larger cage, he started to change.

One day we had company over, so we left Reggie in his cage. He did not like that at all.

He clawed the cage door, letting out his loudest screeches and frantically flapping his wings over and over.

He didn't calm down until we covered the cage with a blanket.

Reggie, the Burrowing Owl

After the company left, we took off the blanket and let Reggie out, just as pleased as pie. We came to realize Reggie just did not like strangers. I guess you could say he was a good "watch owl!"

This next incident happened a few days later. I want to emphasize to children of all ages—never tease an animal, wild or domesticated.

You never know how an animal will respond. We must treat our animal friends with respect; otherwise, we may be hurt or injured. Being teased is something we don't like, and neither do animals.

Bill came home with a couple of his buddies and was excited, to show Reggie to them. Lexie and I had left the house for a while, and when we came back, we caught them teasing Reggie.

They were placing their faces close to his cage and yelling at him. Worst of all , they were trying to poke him with toys and sticks.

The friends were sent home immediately, and Bill went directly to his room for the night. Being teased is how many animals can become mean.

It stresses them out and pushes them beyond their limits until the only thing for them to do is to act out aggressively.

Problems Will Arise—It's a Wild Animal!

I suppose, if that cage door had been open, Reggie would have shown the boys a thing or two.

Another time, Steve was playing with Reggie by throwing a piece of string on the floor and wiggling it in front of him.

When Reggie went to grab for the string, Steve would pull it away. Everything seemed fine for a while. Until suddenly, Reggie grabbed Steve's hand with his beak, closed his eyes, and hung on!

He clawed at Steve's hand while flapping his wings and screeching. Reggie scared Steve more than actually hurting him. All the same, I couldn't take the chance that it might turn into something more.

Reggie, the Burrowing Owl

I had to stop Reggie. I quickly jumped up from my chair. Steve was yelling, "Dad! Help! Make Reggie stop!"

I stood close to them both and shouted, "Stop, Reggie!"

He opened his eyes and looked at me but kept on doing it!

I shouted again, "Stop Reggie!" but this time I included a flick to his beak with my finger. He stopped. He gave me that mean look, made a squawk, and then flew to the curtain rod.

As you can imagine, Steve's hand was scratched up from the claws and had two deep marks from Reggie's beak.

Reggie hadn't hurt Steve badly, but I wondered what would have happened if I hadn't stopped Reggie when I did.

Steve went to clean up his hand and arm and then went outside to play.

I placed some lunch meat in Reggie's cage and tapped on the saucer. I sat down, and within ten minutes Reggie flew over to me, landed on my shoulder, and started his whittling act on my ear lobe and sideburns.

I didn't know what to expect. That was the first time I had to yell and correct Reggie. You should of seen those mean looking eyes of his.

So I just sat still waiting to see what would happen. "Do animals hold grudges like humans?" I wondered.

"Is he going to bite my ear lobe because he's mad at me for scolding him?" Thankfully, he didn't.

It was like nothing happened; he continued to be just as gentle as always. It's both strange and wonderful how animals show affection to humans.

Perhaps this was Reggie's way of apologizing? After a couple of minutes, he flew to his cage and went inside to eat. I quickly walked over and closed the door, and covered the cage. Everything was okay—for a few weeks!

Chapter 12

A Hair-Raising Experience

Whether domesticated or wild, most animals don't typically like sudden, loud noises; not to mention, quick movements.

My aunt Audrey, from Los Angeles, was about to learn this very well. One-day Lexie and I were in the kitchen working, and Reggie watched us while perched atop a kitchen cabinet.

Out of nowhere, my aunt came bursting through the front door and right into the kitchen.

While she was known for her flamboyant behavior, boy, were we ever surprised!

But not as surprised as Reggie and not nearly as surprised as Aunt Audrey was about to be!

Reggie, the Burrowing Owl

"Is anybody home?" she yelled while suddenly appearing in the kitchen.

She received her answer. Reggie gave a loud screech and swooped off the kitchen cabinet, and landed right on my aunt's head!

He pulled and clawed her hair with sharp talons. Aunt Audrey did what any person would do in this situation—take off running and screaming with arms flapping!

Reggie let go of her hair and flew to the curtain rod, giving her a false sense of security for a moment. But just as quick as you could blink, he flew right back and hovered over her head screeching, and flapping his wings.

If it hadn't already, by now complete panic set in. My aunt was waving and shaking her arms above her head, yelling, "Get away from me! Get away from me!"

She flopped to the floor and covered her head with her arms. It happened so fast, but it looked like slow motion in my mind. I ran to my aunt and stood over her, waving my arms to scare Reggie away.

A Hair-Raising Experience

He squawked and flew back to the curtain rod. I was mad, and for the second time in his life, I raised my voice to him. "Get over here Reggie!" I said while slapping his cage.

Amazingly, he flew to his cage and went in. I quickly closed the door and covered the cage.

It took some time for my poor aunt to calm down. She was okay. Reggie hadn't hurt her just scared the peanuts out of her!

I also learned something about Aunt Audrey that day—she'd always been afraid of birds even when they were caged. Yikes!

Reggie, the Burrowing Owl

We left Reggie in his cage, the rest of the day until Aunt Audrey left to go back to Los Angeles. I am sure she had quite the tale to tell her friends. She hadn't known we were raising an owl—now she did!

Chapter 13

The Big Scare

It was a pretty calm and usual morning, if you can call raising a wild burrowing owl in your home, usual. It'd been about a month since the thrilling and hair-raising visit from my aunt. But today's event would prove to be even scarier.

Tom Jr. was now walking, and like Reggie discovering his wings and that he could fly—Tom Jr. discovered he could do more than walk—he could run.

Reggie, the Burrowing Owl

Tom Jr. was all over the place. Up until this time it wasn't unusual to see he and Reggie play together on the carpet. Reggie would land on the floor. Tom Jr. would crawl towards him to try and catch him, but before Tom Jr. could reach Reggie—he'd take off.

Reggie would sit by Tom Jr. on the floor and whittle on his hair. Once Tom Jr. began walking Reggie would perch on his shoulder. He even nestled in his lap to watch TV in the evening and Tom Jr. would tenderly rub Reggie's back until he fell asleep.

These were moments you'd have to see for yourself, to appreciate just how precious they were.

When we say a dog or a cat is a domesticated animal, for the most part, we mean their actions are somewhat predictable.

That is as long as the animal is not mistreated or abused. An abused pet can develop mean tendencies that make it attack the family, but that is the fault of the owners, not the animal.

Although, I remember us having a cat, who for no reason—at least no good reason in my mind—would bite me after I pet her and then she'd run and hide.

The Big Scare

Regardless, with a creature categorized as wild, their behavior can be and is unpredictable, which was the case on this particular day.

Tom Jr. was playing with his toys in the middle of the living room. I was sitting in my favorite chair watching TV. Lexie was in the kitchen, and the rest of the kids were outside. Reggie was playing watchdog perched on the curtain rod.

For reasons I don't know, Tom Jr. jumped up all of a sudden and ran into the kitchen yelling, "Mama!"

I looked at Tom Jr. to see what the commotion was all about. When suddenly, Reggie swooped off the curtain rod and hit Tom Jr. on the left ear with his claw.

Reggie, the Burrowing Owl

Reggie screeched loudly and continued to fly through the kitchen into the entryway, and back to his perch on the curtain rod. Little Tom, was scared and crying and there was a bit of blood where Reggie hit him.

Now, I was really worried. This was the first time Reggie made someone bleed. It could have been little Tom's eye. We cleaned up Tom's ear and gave him a cookie.

There was no point getting angry at Reggie because he was a wild animal and wouldn't understand. Instead, I simply put him in his cage and covered it for the night.

Later in the evening, Lexie and I discussed this and the earlier not-so-pleasant-events that involved Reggie.

Our only conclusions were that he didn't like: strangers, loud noises, children teasing him, or fast movements—like Tom taking off running and yelling.

Therefore, new rules! No longer would we let Reggie fly all over the house all day unless both Lexie and I were in the house to watch the children.

If only one of us was around, then Reggie could only be loose if Tom Jr. was napping.

Now it was too difficult for one person to watch Tom Jr. and Reggie at the same time.

The Big Scare

Likewise, Reggie was no longer our little ball of fuzz; he was a full-grown owl. We were raising a wild bird of prey and we couldn't fault Reggie for being what he was.

All the same, since we couldn't tell if Reggie was only playing or being truly aggressive, we needed to take new measures to protect him and ourselves. We couldn't take any more chances that we might upset Reggie and cause another outburst.

Chapter 14

Reggie at Play

Things were quiet around the house with the new rules. It was an adjustment for us all, and while the family wasn't happy about it, it was hardest on Reggie.

Reggie had been with us for almost one and a half years, and we were used to seeing him fly around the house. Then it all changed.

Reggie, the Burrowing Owl

I'd hear him squawk, and I'd catch myself looking up at the curtain rod to see him, but he was not there. Then I'd remember, he's in his cage!

Reggie often let us know that he wasn't happy in the cage. I was glad we had that big rabbit cage, so he could still flap his wings at least.

He did that often, and he'd also run, jump, and hop around inside.

During the day Lexie let Reggie out while Tom Jr. was taking a nap and the older kids were at school. At night, I let him out once the children were in bed.

It was a sight to see. When I went to his cage, he already knew I was going to let him out.

When I uncovered his cage, he was hanging on the door squawking with excitement.

The second I opened the door he'd fly out and land on my head. Then he'd fly to my shoulder and flap his wings squawking. Next he'd pop on over to Lexie and land on her head. Much to our enjoyment, Reggie repeated his little routine each night when it was just Lexie and me.

My idea of relaxation, after a long day at work was watching television, this was my and Lexie's habit each night. We found Reggie liked watching TV with us.

Reggie At Play

When we turned on the television set, he'd fly down from the curtain rod, and land on my big toe. He had a front-row seat when perched there, and he stared at the TV.

He stood on just one leg, on to my big toe and after a bit, he'd shift to his other leg. Back and forth, back and forth.

During the program, the TV colors changed in brightness. Whenever it happened, Reggie squawked at the TV in response. Then he'd lean a little more toward the TV and squawk again!

And that's how it went most evenings. On a particular night I'm remembering, Reggie was especially entertaining to watch.

We three were watching TV. Reggie was perched on my big toe and started squawking and flapping his wings and squawking some more.

Reggie, the Burrowing Owl

Then he took off for the ceiling, all the while keeping his head cocked to the floor. I looked around to see what the big fuss was.

There wasn't much to see except our oatmeal colored carpet. Then I saw it, a large, dark brown pincher bug crawling on the carpet. Reggie flew to the curtain rod and perched.

He narrowed his gaze and with a loud screech dropped to the floor and snatched the pincher bug right up in his beak. He flew and tried to land on Lexie's head—of all places!

Lexie wanted no part of that! She waved her hands above her head saying, "Go away Reggie! No, stop!"

Reggie took the hint. He wasn't allowed to feast on his catch there, so he flew back to my big toe instead, stood on one leg and devoured his meal.

Another time, I recall one Saturday, Lexie and the kids were gone. I imagine you have heard it said, "When the cat's away the birds will play." Or something like that.

Reggie perched on his favorite spot, the curtain rod, and sat there chatting with me in owl talk. He'd fly to me, nibble my ear, or whittle my hair, or stretch his wings. He certainly needed to do this since he was in the cage most of the day.

Reggie At Play

Well, Reggie and I came up with a neat trick called, "catch the nickel." It started with me pulling out a nickel from my pocket and flipping it in the air to see what he'd do. Reggie sat perched on the curtain rod watching.

He bobbed his head up and down with his eyes staring at the nickel. Finally, I said, "Hey Reggie, get it!" and I flipped it real high and let it fall to the carpet.

Reggie, the Burrowing Owl

He just stared and squawked. I repeated this several times. Finally, when I flipped the nickel up high, Reggie shot like an arrow off the perch and snatched it. But, he couldn't keep a grip on it. It slipped from his claw and fell again to the floor.

I imagine a round flat coin is difficult for an owl to hold in its claws. But no matter, because after a few more tries of flip and grab, Reggie learned to hold on to that nickel!

I don't know, maybe all owls could learn what Reggie did, but to me—he was the smartest bird in the world.

How's this for smart? I could hold my arm out straight in front of me, palm up with a ball of hamburger meat in it and Reggie could zip over and grab that meat without one claw even touching me.

Also, I could hold a piece of baloney in my hand and wave it back and forth. He'd fly to my arm and walk down its length to my hand. When he reached my hand, he'd bend down and grab the baloney with his beak. Then he'd stand back up on one leg and eat his meal on my arm.

Maybe lifting one leg to eat is a form of "reclining" for a bird? I had never raised such an animal before, and I never have since.

Reggie At Play

Reggie was a very good "watch bird." He'd always let us know if we had any visitors at our front door before they could knock or ring the bell.

He also liked elevator music, you know, the soft and gentle music that usually plays while you ride the elevator? Well, they played that kind of music in my time, anyway.

When the kids turned on loud, fast music, he'd squawk and squawk until they turned it off. But soft music put him to sleep.

Reggie learned the hard way about the sliding glass door. One day we had the curtains pulled back, and the sunlight was streaming in just right.

There probably wasn't any reflection, and the outdoors looked quite inviting.

Reggie was flying through the house, and unfortunately, flew right into the glass door. We heard a thud and found poor Reggie standing on the floor and shaking his head.

Thankfully, he was not injured. As I said, he learned the hard way, and he sure never flew into the sliding glass door again!

Chapter 15

Stashing Food and It's a He!

I mentioned before that our only way to get Reggie, into his cage was to entice him with food. Since we weren't letting him out as much as before, we just left the meat inside at the bottom of his cage.

We thought he would help himself to food and we could quickly shut the door. Strangely, there were many times we'd check to see if he was in his cage, so we could close it, and we'd find that the food was gone and there was no sign of Reggie.

Reggie, the Burrowing Owl

Well, we later discovered that this silly owl was stashing his food inside our sofa. He'd crawl under the sofa and climb up inside it through a hole he made! And there he stored his treasures and hid from us.

The little sneak! This presented us with a new problem of how do we stop Reggie from going over to our sofa when he already has a stash of treats to eat?

We had to stop leaving food inside his cage so his supply in the couch would run out. Then, we could once again bribe him with food. I know what you're thinking, "What if we sat on the sofa with Reggie inside and squashed him?"

Well, remember, we didn't let him out of his cage unless both of us were there to supervise. Most of the time it was just Lexie and me. We always made sure we didn't sit on the sofa when Reggie was out of his cage. Before sitting down, we checked to see if he was on either the curtain rod or in the kitchen on one of the cabinets.

One night we finally concluded that Reggie was for certain a he and not a she, and it was Lexie who discovered it!

All the kids were in bed, and Lexie and I were still up . Reggie was inside his little fort— our sofa—making cute cooing noises.

Stashing Food and It's a He!

I was in the living room, and Lexie was in the dining room ironing.

Every time Reggie went "cucoo-oo", Lexie answered back by also going "cucoo-oo".

Each time Lexie responded with a "cucoo-oo", Reggie came charging out from under the sofa and stared at Lexie. If she didn't say "cucoo-oo", he'd dart back under the sofa and start to "cucoo-oo cucoo-oo" from under there.

It went on for several minutes. Okay, so now Reggie was again inside his fort, making these cooing sounds and again Lexie was answering him.

Suddenly, Reggie came busting out and ran, not flew, over to the ironing board cord and jumped on it. He moved his wings up and down and let out a squawk, then turned and ran back under the sofa.

Reggie continued, to "cucoo-oo" but they were slower and not as frequent. Lexie decided to kick it up a notch, and she responded to Reggie with "cucoo-oo."

Now with her encouragement, Reggie started again, and this cucoo-ooing went back and forth until I was ready to tear my hair out!

But then "it" happened! Reggie came back out from under the sofa and stood still. He puffed his feathers up, which made his body look twice its size.

Next, he bent over with his head aimed directly at Lexie. With his wings stretched out wide and body bent low, he began a steady march towards Lexie.

His eyes looked mean, and he kept the cucoo-ooing coming. "Honey, please make him stop! I think he is going to attack me!" Lexie yelled.

I went and stood in between Reggie and Lexie. I couldn't help but laugh! Reggie wasn't going to attack Lexie—he was trying to woo her! And I interrupted his romance.

Stashing Food and It's A He!

Well, that must have made him mad. He looked up at me, let out a loud screech, ruffled his feathers and ran back under the sofa. He continued to softly coo, but Lexie decided it was a good idea not to answer back anymore. So, the unfortunate love bird eventually stopped. I can say that Lexie never responded with "cucoo-oo" to Reggie again!

Folks, I don't know a whole lot about the mating patterns of animals, but I have heard that it's usually the male that initiates courtship.

There was no doubt that what normally happened in the wild unfolded in my own home. From what I saw and heard, I could only conclude that Reggie was looking for a date. But not my wife —"geez!"

Chapter 16

Where There is Smoke, There is Fire

We don't think bad things, that happen to others, can happen to us until they do.

A fire occurred in our home. Fortunate for us, it was isolated to one room and by the time the fire trucks arrived I had put it out, using a garden hose.

Thankfully, it was caught in time and didn't consume the whole house, but what a mess.

Reggie, the Burrowing Owl

There was a thick black smoke that hovered throughout the lower level of the house. It started from the ceiling to two feet above the floor. This air gap was just above Reggie's cage so the smoke, thank goodness, did not reach him.

The firemen placed a blower unit in the bedroom window, that did a fine job of drawing the smoke out of the house.

The only rooms downstairs without smoke damage were Debbie's and Linda's because their doors had been shut.

For the next three weeks, we kept Reggie's cage in Debbie's room during the day until the repair work was complete. There wasn't any carpet in Debbie's room, and we were concerned, it might be too damp for him.

Where There is Smoke, There is Fire

Each night, when all the children were in bed, I went into Debbie's room and brought Reggie to the living room and let him out of his cage.

I imagine our poor Reggie wasn't happy with all the changes that were taking place. It must have been a lot for one creature to handle.

For a year and a half, Reggie had always been able to enjoy the front living room, be around people, listen to and watch TV, and play with Tom Jr.

Those were his familiar surroundings and his daily routines. Now, he was in an unfamiliar area of the house, with a cold floor, a small window, and little door. He was all by himself for most of the day, until the house repairs were complete.

At first, we tried to let him stay in the cage out in the living room, but he'd squawk and screech all day, at the workers.

Plus, his cage was large and in the way of their work. The fire made it very miserable for all of us, but mostly for Reggie.

I let him out as soon as I came home from work and the repairmen had left. He always immediately flew to the curtain rod, but there was no curtain rod anymore. We took it down due to smoke damage.

Reggie, the Burrowing Owl

He'd check everything out and let out a few squawks, flying between the living, dining, and kitchen areas several times.

The first week after the fire, Reggie wasn't himself, and he barely ate. Since he wasn't interested in food, it was difficult to settle him down at night.

I had to catch him and place him in his cage. Reggie's lack of interest in food was worrying all of us. But we hoped for the best and that our world would return to normal as soon as the repair work was completed.

Thankfully by the second week of repair, Reggie appeared to be his old self again.

When I carried his cage into the living room, he'd perch happily on the door, flapping his wings and squawking.

One night after we let him out, he flew to Lexie, landed on her shoulder, and began whittling her hair.

She, talked to him saying "Hi baby! Are you happy out here with us?" He then dropped into her lap, and she stroked him like a kitten.

His big eyes closed, and he let out those cute little chirp-chirp sounds. Then he came to me for the same attention. We made small balls of hamburger and fed them to him while he snuggled in our laps.

Where There is Smoke, There is Fire

It was quite a sight to see this wild owl being tame and showing affection. If I hadn't experienced it, I wouldn't have believed it.

After three weeks of restoration, the house was finally back in order, with a fresh, clean carpet. Our home smelled brand new, and we were all happy the nightmare was over!

Chapter 17

Our Loss, Heaven's Gain

It was Friday night, and we were celebrating. The house was back in order, and we felt great. Steve and I carried Reggie's cage out one last time from Debbie's room. We set it back in the living room on the floor.

"There you go Reggie, back where you belong!" I said pleased.

He looked up at me and squawked as if to say, "You better believe it and do not let it happen again!"

Looking back, I am glad I decided to let Reggie out of his cage with all the children around that night. Each one wanted to play with him.

It was good to see him flying around, landing on shoulders, giving little kisses, and whittling everyone's hair. He even jumped to the floor where Tom Jr. and Bill were playing. It was just like when Reggie first arrived.

Reggie, the Burrowing Owl

There were feelings of love and togetherness. We loved Reggie with all our hearts, and there was and still is no way to describe what it is like for a whole family to care for and enjoy such a beautiful creature together.

I said, "Let's see how Reggie acts over the next couple days. If everything goes okay, maybe he won't have to be in his cage all the time."

When I said that, everyone just lit up with joy. You'd think I'd just doubled their allowances.

It was turning out to be a wonderful Friday evening. I noticed Reggie did seem to have a little trouble flying and he was sneezing from time to time. None of this stopped him from playing with the children, or with Lexie and me.

Sadly, the evening came to an end, and Lexie said, "Hey troops, time for bed! Tomorrow is another day, and poor Reggie looks pooped!"

In unison, the children cried, "Oh, do we have too? It's too early still, just a little longer."

Their cries didn't work, and with a final, "Now!" they all marched to bed, and Lexie tucked in Tom Jr.

Our Loss, Heaven's Gain

After that, it was just Lexie, Reggie and I for a little longer. It sure felt good to let him out again. Reggie perched on my big toe watching TV and whittling his feathers like always. Lexie came in with his food and water and placed them in his cage. He walked up from my big toe along my leg and into my lap.

I stroked the top of his head, and under his beak for a few minutes. He closed his eyes. I gently picked him up, and he didn't fight me.

He just opened his eyes a little, let out a small chirp, and closed them again. I walked over to his cage and set him inside.

He hopped up onto his perch and let out a squawk as if to say, "Good night!". And then he closed his eyes.

"Reggie sure looks tired," I said to Lexie. She agreed softly and placed the cover over the cage.

"Good night Reggie," I said, and the two of us went upstairs to bed.

I hardly slept, I was a worried about, Reggie. Something didn't feel right when we put him to bed. My fears were sadly confirmed, when a loud cry woke Lexie and me with a start.

"Mom! Dad! Something's wrong with Reggie!"

Reggie, the Burrowing Owl

We shot up and ran downstairs, to Reggie's cage. The cover was already pulled off, and Reggie was standing there on one leg.

One claw clutched the bottom of the cage, and the other leg was drawn up to his body. He had one eye open and one eye closed. His little body leaned against a corner of the cage.

I opened the doors and touched him. He was stiff and still. He didn't move.

With my heart in my throat, I slowly turned and looked into the children's tear-streamed faces. They knew before I said it. "Our little Reggie is gone!"

Our Loss, Heaven's Gain

Then Lexie and I teared up. I tried clearing my throat to say something that would comfort us all, but I couldn't find any words.

For what felt like hours, no one could do anything, but stare at Reggie.

We couldn't believe he was gone. I turned to Lexie and asked if she had a white cloth to wrap Reggie in.

She left to go get the cloth, and one of the kids said, "We were just playing with him last night."

"What could have happened to him?" said another. All these emotions and no answers to our questions, as to what happened.

We would never know, but even if we did, it could never change the extreme sadness we shared over this loss.

We had been brought together as a family by Reggie's life and now again in his death.

Lexie returned with the cloth. As I worked to free Reggie's foot off the cage floor, I had a hard time keeping back tears.

I often feel like I am reliving that sad moment again. It just wasn't right, I thought, as constant questions about what occurred flooded my mind.

But it was too late. Nothing could change what had already happened.

Reggie, the Burrowing Owl

I finally freed Reggie's foot, and carefully wrapped him in the clean white cloth.

Lexie, through swollen tear-filled eyes, said, "What are you going to do Tom?"

"I'll tell you what I'm going to do and we're going to do it as a family. We will bury little Reggie in our back yard!"

I found an empty three-pound peanut butter jar with the lid and carefully placed him inside. I put the lid on tight, then wrapped electrical tape around it.

All the children were still crying, their faces sad and long as I finished taping the jar.

I cleared my throat and said, "There, that should keep Reggie safe from bugs and ants. Everyone needs to dress up and then we will find a resting place for him!"

Soon, we all met in the back yard to look for the perfect spot. There was a hill along the entire back section of the yard, with a high fence that blocked the freeway.

I had planted a lot of palm trees there, and green ground cover grew over most of the hill.

We all agreed the spot should be under the biggest palm tree. It was a beautiful spot, with large rocks on each side of the tree. So, I dug between the rocks, and when the hole was deep enough, I stopped and picked up the jar.

Our Loss, Heaven's Gain

I cleared my throat, and I let the tears flow freely. I spoke, "We give you Reggie, our loss and heaven's gain. Reggie has given the whole family, joy, warmth, responsibility, and the opportunity to live with one of God's beautiful creatures. We will never forget him!"

Then I laid Reggie to rest at the base of the palm tree. There wasn't a single dry eye.

Chapter 18

Reggie Perched in the Trees - An Epilogue

After our little memorial service for Reggie, we somberly marched one by one back into the house. Each of us slumped down in the nearest available seat in the living room.

As I looked around, I noticed we had formed a semi-circle around Reggie's cage. There was a weight to the emptiness of his cage, and it settled on our hearts.

In turn, we shared what we missed about Reggie.

It was going to be hard not seeing him flying freely around the house and perching on his favorite place—the curtain rod.

I said, "Sometimes life seems too short. If Steve had not found and brought Reggie home his life would probably have been even shorter, but of course, we don't know that for certain.

"However, we do know, that we had the opportunity of a lifetime, to care for an animal that most families could only dream about, or never think of caring for."

"We will always love and miss the little owl we raised from a baby," said Lexie.

Reggie Perched in the Trees - An Epilogue

As we continued to talk about Reggie, Lexie and I could sense the children's sadness lightening a little. Their shoulders relaxed, and their heads didn't hang so low.

"I tell you what," I said, "I'll make a little headstone out of wood, and in a few days, we'll have another ceremony in Reggie's honor, as we place it where he now lays."

A few days later, Lexie took out the green ground cover and planted a flowering type over Reggie's resting spot. She formed it in the shape of a heart and when it bloomed, there were reddish-pink flowers, with one yellow flower in the center.

The headstone was ready, so we called the children together. It was painted white, with black letters that read, "REGGIE."

I made another little speech and said, "Our beloved Reggie, now free to fly and perch outside!" While all the children watched, I set Reggie's headstone in place.

"Dad," Steve remarked, "Reggie never did live outside or fly among the trees."

"You're right son, but I thought it might be better for us to remember him, as he could of been, living outdoor and free to perch on tree limbs and bushes!"

The children all nodded their heads in agreement.

Reggie, the Burrowing Owl

As time went on, things returned to "normal" as they should, but we never forgot that sweet ball of fuzz.

The children are grown now and have their own families. Tom Jr. passed away in 1996 and Lexie passed away in 2010.

As of more recent, I have been working with my son, Derrick, who has helped me re-write this story. As I read it now, I feel as though I have gone back in time.

It is good to remember and reflect on the adventures we had together with that fearless and charming little owl. I hope by sharing this story, it allowed you to join us in the adventure!

If you wish to learn more about owls, there are plenty of resources available, unlike what I had in the 1960s with only our handy encyclopedia set. (I highly recommend you thumb through a copy if you ever have the opportunity.)

If you find a stray or injured bird, please seek help for it. We have included a list of government agencies and other resources. Also check with your local State and County agencies for bird or raptor refuges and shelters that assist stray and wild animals by caring for, rehabilitating and releasing the birds if they are able.

Reggie Perched in the Trees - An Epilogue

Now, as more rural areas continue to grow into cities, owls and other wild animals that once lived in the surrounding areas have been pushed out and find it hard to survive. In the United States, many states deem the burrowing owl "a species of concern."

Stay informed and find out what you can do to help. Visit our website at ReggieTheOwl.com We invite child 6- 16 to join *Reggie's Adventure Club*.

Resources

All About Birds:
www.allaboutbirds.org/guide/Burrowing_Owl/id

Audubon: www.adudon.org/field-guide/bird/ burrowing-owl

Burrowing Owl Conservation Network:
www.burrowingowlconservation.org

National Wildlife Federation:
nwf.org/Wildlife/Wildlife-Library/Birds/Burrowing-Owl.aspx

Saskatchewan Burrowing Owl Interp. Centre:
skburrowingowl.ca

Wild At Heart Raptors - An Arizona-based raptor rescue organization: wildatheartraptors.org

We wish you much happiness and enjoyment,
Thomas J. Wood and Derrick J. Wood

Made in the USA
Coppell, TX
30 January 2021

49180624R00073